Super Cheap Prague Travel Guide 2019

Our Mission

Travel guides show you pricey accommodation and restaurants because they make money OFF OF YOU. Travel bloggers and influencers often do the same. Super Cheap Guides help you use the system against itself to experience unforgettable trips that will blow your mind, not your budget.

We believe that travel can and is best enjoyed on a budget. We work to dispel myths, save you tons of money and help you find experiences that will flash before your eyes when you come to take your last breath on this beautiful earth.

Perhaps the biggest money saving trick you can employ is to know what you want to spend on and what you don't. This guide focuses on the cheap or free, but we do include the unique things to experience in our worth the fee section. There is little value in travelling somewhere and not experiencing all it has to offer. Where possible we've included cheap workarounds.

We are the first travel guide company to include Airbnb's in our recommendations if you think any of these need updating you can email me at philgtang@gmail.com

Who this book is for and why anyone can enjoy budget travel

Friends and family always ask me 'How can you afford to travel?' my response 'I have a unique skill and passion for finding bargains'. This doesn't mean I do any less or sleep in dirty hostels. Someone who spends A LOT on travel hasn't planned or wants to spend their money. I have formulated a system - which I hope to pass on to you in my travel guides - to juice everything from my travel adventures while spending the least possible money.

There is a difference between being cheap and frugal - I like to spend money on beautiful experiences, but 18 years of travel has taught me I could have a 20 cent experience that will stir my soul more than a $100 one. Of course, there are times when the reverse is true, my point is, spending money on travel is the best investment you can make but it doesn't have to be at levels set by hotels and attractions with massive ad spends and influencers who are paid small fortunes to get you to buy into something that you could have for a fraction of the cost.

Talking of 'the gram'. I've never used it, and probably never will though I have many friends who text me when they find good discounts on it or Twitter/Facebook, I love travelling so much because it forces me to be present-minded. I like to have the cold hard budget busting facts to hand (which is why I've included so many one page charts), but otherwise, I want to shape my own experience - and I'm sure you do too.

I have designed these travel guides to give you a unique planning tool to experience a soul-stirring trip without spending the ascribed tourist budget.

When it comes to FUN budget travel, it's all about what you know. You can have all the feels without most of the bills. An hour spent planning can save you hundreds on the same, maybe even thousands on the same experiences. Super Cheap Insider Guideshave done the planning for you, so you can focus on what matters: immersing yourself in the sights, sounds and smells, meeting awesome people and most importantly, being relaxed and happy. My sincere hope is that my tips will bring you great joy at a fraction of the price most people recommend.

So, grab a cup of tea, put your feet up and relax; you're about to enter the world of enjoying Prague on the cheap. Oh and don't forget a biscuit. You need energy to plan a trip of a lifetime on a budget.

Super Cheap Prague is <u>not</u> for travellers with the following needs:

1. You require a book with detailed offline travel maps. Super Cheap Guides are best used with Google Maps - download before you travel to make the most of your time and money.
2. You would like thousands of accommodation, food and attraction recommendations; by definition, cheapest is most often singular. We only include maximum value recommendations. We purposively leave out over-priced attractions when there is no workaround.
3. You would like detailed write-ups about hotels/Airbnbs/Restaurants. We are bargain hunters first and foremost. We dedicate our time to finding the best deals, not writing flowery language about their interiors. Plus things change. If I had a pound for every time I read a Lonely Planet description only to find the place totally different, I would be a rich man. Always look at online reviews for the latest up to date information.

If you want to save A LOT of money while comfortably enjoying an unforgettable trip to Prague, minus the marketing, hype, scams and tourist traps read on.

Congratulations, you're saving money and doing Good!

We donate 10% of all book profits to charity.

This year we are donating to Animal Shelters including one in Prague. The number of abandoned and homeless dogs and cats in Europe is over 100 million - the problem is particularly bad in the eastern and southern parts of Europe. I'm sure you've seen your fair share of abandoned dogs during your travels: its heart wrenching to see man's best friend starving and alone.

'My dog Gracie was abandoned on the highway in Slovakia. At just ten months old, they tied her to the railings and left her there. Animal Hope picked her up and took care of her and found her a home with us. She is now a healthy, happy girl and loves travelling with us, getting her nose into new smells and soliciting belly rubs from fellow travellers. What breaks my heart is her 'I haven't been abandoned dance'. She is always so happy that we haven't abandoned her when we collect her from outside a supermarket that she dances on her leash for several minutes. Watch her 'I haven't been abandoned dance' dance   . Money could never buy the happiness she has brought my family and me, but donations can help other abandoned animals like her to find loving homes.'

Katherine Huber, a contributor to Super Cheap Vienna.

Donations are made on the 4th January of each year on profits from the previous year. To nominate a charity to receive 10% of the proceeds of sales from our 2020 editions complete the form here: supercheapinsiderguides.com

Gracie

Redefining Super Cheap

I grew up thinking you had to spend more than you could afford to have a good time travelling. Now I've visited many countries I know nothing is further from the truth. Before you embark upon reading our specific tips for Prague. I want you to think about what you associate with the word cheap because you make your beliefs and your beliefs make you.

Here are the dictionary definitions of cheap:

1. costing very little; relatively low in price; inexpensive:
a cheap dress.
2. costing little labor or trouble:
Words are cheap.
3. charging low prices:
a very cheap store.
4. **of little account; of small value; mean; shoddy:**
cheap conduct; cheap workmanship.
5. **embarrassed; sheepish:**
He felt cheap about his mistake.
6. **stingy; miserly:**
He's too cheap to buy his own brother a cup of coffee.

Three out of six definitions have extremely negative connotations. The 'super cheap' we're talking about in this book is not shoddy, embarrassed or stingy. Hey, you've already donated to charity just by buying this book - how is that stingy? We added the super to reinforce our message. Super's dictionary definition stands for 'a super quality'. Super Cheap stands for enjoying the best on the lowest budget. Question other peoples definitions of cheap so you're not blinded to possibilities, potential, and prosperity. Here are some new associations to consider forging:

Shoddy

Cheap stuff doesn't last is an adage marketing companies have drilled into consumers. However by asking vendors the right questions cheap doesn't mean something won't last, I had a $10 backpack last for 8 years and a $100 suitcase bust on the first journey. A   out of San Francisco University found that people who spent money on experiences rather than things were happier. Memories last forever, not things, even expensive things. And as we will show you during this guide you don't need to pay to create great memories.

Embarrassed

I have friends who routinely pay more to vendors because they think their money is putting food on this person's table. Paradoxically, Cuban doctors are driving taxi's because they earn more money; it's not always a good thing for the place you're visiting to pay more and can cause unwanted distortion in their culture - Airbnb pushing out renters is an obvious example. Think carefully about whether the extra money is helping people or incentivising greed.

Stingy

Cheap can be eco-friendly. Buying thrift clothes is cheap but you also help the Earth. Many travellers are often disillusioned by the reality of traveling experience since the places on our bucketlists are overcrowded. Cheap can take you away from the crowds. You can find balance and harmony being cheap. Remember, "A journey is best measured in friends, rather than miles." – Tim Cahill. And making friends is free!

Discover Prague

St Charles Bridge

The ruling Přemyslid dynasty moved their family seat to
Prague founding the city in the 9th century, but settlers pre-date
the Palaeolithic period - 2.58 million years ago!

Prague is a city that has survived being pulled in all directions. It
was part of the Holy Roman Empire (Habsburgs dynasty) and
lastly the Eastern communist bloc. Today it is an enchanting mix
of the old and new. The Nové Mesto (New Town) is a symbol of
the new independent Czech Republic, while the Staré Mesto (Old
Town) remained untouched in both World Wars displaying 1000
years of Prague in all its glory.

Prague offers a wealth of opportunities to experience the city for
free, from strolls through the city streets soaking up the spectacu-
lar medieval and gothic architecture to a number of free museums, delicious cheap beers, parks and churches, as well as fabu-
lous free entertainment. If you follow the advice in this guide you

could easily have the time of your life in Prague for $30 a day including accommodation.

INSIDER CULTURAL INSIGHT

Andrej Babis was elected prime minister of the Czech Republic in December 2017. His populist politics, outlandish style and exuberant wealth have earnt him the nickname the Czech Donald Trump.

Planning your trip

When to visit?
If you are not tied to school holidays, the best time to visit is during the shoulder-season months mid-April to May and September to mid-October the weather is convenient for sightseeing and the crowds are yet to arrive.

Where to stay?
Stay within 20 minutes walk of Prague's old Town. It's easy and cheap to get around Prague but the best way to explore the city is to walk.

The cheapest place to stay
You can get a dorm bed for $10 a night and I've heard great things about Mad House hostel, Sir Toby's, Czech Inn and Downtown hostel.

Airbnbs offer a better price/ performance ratio, especially if you're not a solo traveller. I stayed in an entire apartment for $9 a night - https://www.airbnb.com/rooms/8965964?s=51 It is not so expensive to eat out in Prague, as long as you don't choose touristy places so you won't save much cooking at home but its nice to be able to make yourself a cup of tea especially if you braved St Charles Bridge in rush hour.

Hack your Prague Accommodation

Your two biggest expenses when travelling to Prague are accommodation and food. This section is intended to help you cut these costs dramatically before and while you are in Prague.

Hostels are the cheapest accommodation in Prague but there are some creative workarounds to upgrade your stay on the cheap.

Use Time

There are two ways to use time. One is to book in advance. Three months will net you the best deal, especially if your visit coincides with an event. The other is to book on the day of your stay. This is a risky move, but if executed well, you can lay your head in a five-star hotel for a 2-star fee.

Before I travelled to Prague, I checked for big events using a simple google search 'What's on in Prague', there were no big events drawing travellers so I risked showing up with no accommodation booked (If there are big events on demand exceeds supply and you should avoid using this strategy) I started checking for discount rooms at 11 am using a private browser on booking.com.

Before I go into demand-based pricing, take a moment to think about your risk tolerance. By risk, I am not talking about personal safety. No amount of financial savings is worth risking that. What I am talking about is being inconvenienced. Do you deal well with last-minute changes? Can you roll with the punches or do you dislike it if something changes? Everyone is different and knowing yourself is the best way to plan a great trip. If you are someone that likes to have everything pre-planned using demand-based pricing to get cheap accommodation will not work for you. Skip this section and go to blind-booking.

Demand-based pricing

Be they an Airbnb host or hotel manager; no one wants empty rooms. Most will do anything to make some revenue because they still have the same costs to cover whether the room is occupied or not. That's why you will find many hotels drastically slashing room rates for same-day bookings.

How to book five-star hotels for a two-star price

You will not be able to find these discounts when the demand exceeds the supply. So if you're visiting during the peak season, or during an event which has drawn many travellers don't try this.

On the day of your stay, visit booking.com (which offers better discounts than Kayak and agoda.com). Hotel Tonight individually checks for any last-minute bookings, but they take a big chunk of the action, so the better deals come from booking.com. The best results come from booking between 2 pm and 4 pm when the risk of losing any revenue with no occupancy is most pronounced, so algorithms supporting hotels slash prices. This is when you can find rates that are not within the "lowest publicly visible" rate. To avoid losing customers to other websites, or cheapening the image of their hotel most will only offer the super cheap rates during a two hour window from 2 pm to 4 pm. Two guests will pay 10x difference in price but it's absolutely vital to the hotel that neither knows it.

Takeaway: To get the lowest price book on the day of stay between 2 pm and 4 pm and extend your search radius to include further afield hotels with good transport connections.

How to trick travel Algorithms to get the lowest hotel price

Do not believe anyone who says changing your IP address to get cheaper hotels or flights does NOT work. If you don't believe us, download a Tor Network and search for flights and hotels to one destination using your current IP and then the tor network (a tor browser hits your IP address from algorithms. It is commonly used by hackers). You will receive different prices.

The price you see is a decision made by an algorithm that adjusts prices using data points such as past bookings, remaining capacity, average demand and the probability of selling the room or flight later at a higher price. If booking.com knows you've searched for the area before it will keep the prices high. To circumvent this, you can either use a different IP address from a cafe or airport or data from an international sim. I use a sim from Three, which provides free data in many countries around the world. When you search from a new IP address, most of the time, and particularly near booking you will get a lower price. Sometimes if your sim comes from a 'rich' country, say the UK or USA, you will see higher rates as the algorithm has learnt people from these countries pay more. The solution is to book from a local wifi connection - but a different one from the one you originally searched from.

How to get last-minute discounts on owner rented properties

In addition to Airbnb, you can also find owner rented rooms and apartments on www.vrbo.com or HomeAway or a host of others. Nearly all owners renting accommodation will happily give renters a "last-minute" discount to avoid the space sitting empty, not earning a dime.

Go to Airbnb or another platform and put in today's date. Once you've found something you like start the negotiating by asking for a 25% reduction. A sample message to an Airbnb host might read:

Dear HOST NAME,

I love your apartment. It looks perfect for me. Unfortunately, I'm on a very tight budget. I hope you won't be offended, but I wanted to ask if you would be amenable to offering me a 25% discount for tonight, tomorrow and the following day? I see that you aren't booked. I can assure you, I will leave your place exactly the way I found it. I will put bed linen in the washer and ensure everything is clean for the next guest. I would be delighted to bring you a bottle of wine to thank you for any discount that you could offer.

If this sounds okay, please send me a custom offer, and I will book straight away.

YOUR NAME.

In my experience, a polite, genuine message like this, that proposes reciprocity will be successful 80% of the time. Don't ask for more than 25% off, this person still has to pay the bills and will probably say no as your stay will cost them more in bills than they make. Plus starting higher, can offend the owner and do you want to stay somewhere, where you have offended the host?

In Practice

To use either of these methods, you must travel light. Less stuff means greater mobility, everything is faster and you don't have to check-in or store luggage. If you have a lot of luggage, you're going to have fewer of these opportunities to save on accommodation. Plus travelling light benefits the planet - you're buying, consuming, and transporting less stuff.

Blind-booking

If your risk tolerance does not allow for last-minute booking, you can use blind-booking. Many hotels not wanting to cheapen their brand with known low-prices, choose to operate a blind booking policy. This is where you book without knowing the name of the hotel you're going to stay in until you've made the payment. This is also sometimes used as a marketing strategy where the hotel is seeking to recover from past issues. I've stayed in plenty of blind book hotels. As long as you choose 4 or 5 star hotels, you will find them to be clean, comfortable and safe. priceline.com, Hot Rate® Hotels and Top Secret Hotels (operated by lastminute.com) offer the best deals.

Hotels.com Loyalty Program

This is currently the best hotel loyalty program with hotels in Prague. The basic premise is you collect 10 nights and get 1 free. hotels.com price match, so if booking.com has a cheaper price you can get hotel.com, to match. If you intend to travel more than ten nights in a year, its a great choice to get the 11th free.

Don't let time use you.

Rigidity will cost you money. You pay the price you're willing to pay, not the amount it requires a hotel to deliver. Therefore if you're in town for a big event, saving money on accommodation is nearly impossible so in such cases book three months ahead.

The best price performance location in Prague

A room putting Prague's attractions, restaurants, and nightlife within walking distance will save you time on transport. You could walk around the corner from a main attraction and find cheaper restaurants and bars off the main stretch so you don't need to stay miles out for cheap beers and food. You will get a better idea of the day to day life of a local if you stay in a neighbourhood like Mala Strana (Little Quarter). It depends on the Prague you want to experience. For the tourist experience stay in the centre 20 minutes walk from St Charles Bridge, either in a last-minute hotel or Airbnb. For a taste of local life the hip district of Mala Strana (Little Quarter) is the best you will find. Vyšehrad Castle Suite is a luxurious four-star hotel with consistent last-minute rooms from $40 a night.

Saving money on Prague Food

Breakfast

If you stay somewhere with a free breakfast, eat smart. Don't eat sugary cereals or white flour rich pastries if you don't want to be hungry an hour later. Before leaving your hotel or checking out, find some fresh fruit, water, and granola in the fitness centre or coffee in the lobby or business centre. If your hotel doesn't have free breakfast, don't take it. You can always eat cheaper outside. Bohemia Bagel (address: Lázeňská 282/19) has the best cheap breakfast we found. Here you can pick up Bagels for less than $2.

Visit supermarkets at discount times.

You can get a 50 per cent discount around 5 pm at the Billa or Tesco supermarkets on fresh produce. The cheaper the super-market, the less discounts you will find, so check Billa or Tesco before the discount markets at 5 pm. Some items are also marked down due to sell-by date after the lunchtime rush so its also worth to check in around 3 pm.

Use delivery services on the cheap.

Take advantage of local offers on food delivery services. Most platforms including Uber Eats and Delivery Hero offer $10 off the first order in Prague.

SNAPSHOT: How to enjoy a $1,000 trip to Prague for $100

(full breakdown at the end of the guide)

Stay	Entire apartment $9 in the centre https://www.airbnb.com/rooms/8965964?s=51
Eat	Beer, Trdelník (rolled pastries). Sausages (Klobásy), Česnečka (garlic soup), Guláš (goulash)
Move	Walk and use the subway. $5
See	St Charles Bridge, churches, Palace and the Prague Castle
Total	US$100

Unique bargains I love in Prague

Prague is an outdoor museum of Renaissance, baroque, neo-classical, art nouveau and modern architecture where beer flows cheaper than water. In most eateries beer is cheaper than bottled water. Tap water is safe here, so fill your water bottle up carefree and enjoy your cheap beer to. Eating out is surprisingly cheap (when you avoid places near the main sites). Cafes are abundant and cheap: Skautský institut or Dobrá trafika cafés. Slightly more hipster cafés and food: AntHill, Kavárna co hledá jméno, Mammacoffee, Cafefin, Cafe Neustadt, Globe bookstore and café. If you love cheese definitely try Raclettka - they have awesome French Raclette and Swiss fondue for $5.

The glorious architecture is all free, as is the street entertainment on Charles Bridge. Without having to buy a ticket, you can wander through the courtyards and gardens of Prague Castle and watch the centuries old changing of the guard ceremony. Prague is a bargain hunters paradise when you know where to look. The first thing you should do when you arrive is check https://www.facebook.com/groups/FreeEventsInPrague/ to see what free events are on.

NOTE: Most public toilets in Prague they ask for 50 cents. Use the toilet at your accommodation and in public buildings to avoid flushing your money away. Men's toilets are marked Muži and women's zeny or damy.

How to use this book

Google and Tripadvisor are your on-the-go guides while travelling, a travel guide adds the most value during the planning phase, and if you're without wifi. Always download the google map for your destination - having an offline map will make using this guide much more comfortable. For ease of use, we've set the book out the way you travel starting with arriving, how to get around, then on to the money-saving tips. The tips we ordered according to when you need to know the tip to save money, so free tours and combination tickets feature first. We prioritised the rest of the tips by how much money you can save and then by how likely it was that you would be able to find the tip with a google search. Meaning those we think you could find alone are nearer the bottom. I hope you find this layout useful. If you have any ideas about making super cheap guides easy to use, please email me philgattang@gmail.com. Now let's started with juicing the most pleasure from your trip to Prague with the least possible money.

Our Super Cheap Tips

Arriving

The cheapest way to get to Prague city center from the airport is bus. The bus station is right in front of the Terminal 2 (Exit D). A ticket valid for 90 minutes costs €1.25 (32 CZK) and you can use it for the bus, tram or subway. Just take the bus 119 to Nadrazi Veleslavin where you must transfer to subway line A (green) and you can continue to downtown (Mustek) or any other station.

Getting around

Bike

Prague is a lovely city to cycle. Like a growing number of cities around the world, Prague has a bike-sharing program, https://www.rekola.cz/en/ averaging a $1 per 30 minutes, but free for the first 15 minutes. So if you only do short trips, you can cycle for free during your time in Prague.

Public transport

As lovely as it is to roam the cobbled streets of the Old Town and cross Charles Bridge to the sound of buskers, you may need to use Prague's public transport. When you do, buy day/multi-tickets. A day-long ticket costs 70Kc, and a 3-day ticket will set you back 200Kc - $8USD, saving you money. The tourist attractions are dotted along line A - the green line. There are also trams, which are a lovely way to see Prague. Line 22 goes to the Prague Castle and other attractions.

Start with a free walking tour

The Dancing House

Forget exploring Prague by wandering around aimlessly. Start with a free organised tour. Nothing compares to local advice, especially when travelling on a budget. Ask for their recommendations for the best cheap eats, the best bargains, the best markets, the best place for a particular street eat. Perhaps some of it will be repeated from this guide, but it can't hurt to ask, especially if you have specific needs or questions. At the end you should leave an appropriate tip (usually around $5), but nobody bats an eye lid if you are unable or unwilling to do so, tell them you will leave a good review and always give them a little gift from home - I always carry small Vienna fridge magnets (because thats where I live) and I always tip the $5, but it is totally up to you.

This is the free tour I did. I thought it was a great introduction to the city and covered all the main attractions. You can book here: http://www.neweuropetours.eu/prague

A note on paying for tours

The only time paying for a tour is worth it, is when you couldn't reach the place without the tour (e.g you need a boat), or when the tour is about the same price as the attraction entry. Otherwise you can do a range of self-guided tours using gpsmycity.com for FREE.

Consider the Prague Card

Attraction aficionados can save money with a Prague Card in advance, you can buy it online and collect the card at the airport or at the city center. For 52 euros you get free access to 50 attractions in Prague, including the Castle, the Old Town Hall and many more. Plus free public transportation and free shuttle bus from Prague Airport to city center. Personally I didn't buy it because the attractions are quite cheap around $10 each, but if you're planning a longer trip to see more attractions it might be right for you.

Watch Sunrise at St Charles Bridge

St Charles bridge is the most iconic tourist attraction in Prague. Built during the 14th and 15th century to connect the Old Town and Lesser Town (Malá Strana). Legend has it egg yolks were mixed into the mortar to strengthen the construction of the bridge. While crossing the bridge pay attention to the sculptures, the beautiful Vltava River and climb one of the towers, the view from the top is amazing. Make sure you visit at sunrise, 4:30 - 5:30am, its magical without the crowds.

INSIDER HISTORICAL INSIGHT

Touch the statue of St. John of Nepomuk- it is said it will bring you good luck.

Visit museums for free

The National Museum

To make sure everybody has access to culture many of Pragues top museums are free on specific days (these days have been cut by 50% in the last 5 years - so plan your trip to maximise savings) and ALL are worth a visit. Here are the best of the crop:

- National Museum on the first Monday of the month.
- Most of the main galleries on the first Tuesday of the month.
- Prague City Museum on the first Thursday of the month.

The Kafka Museum named after one of the greatest writers of the 20th century who was from Prague is worth the fee. Pay 180Kc - $7 if you are interested to learn more about his life and his work.

Visit Valdstejnsky Palace (Wallenstein Palace)

Valdstejnsky Palace

Visit this FREE palace in the Lesser Town. Built between 1624 and 1630, it comprises twenty three houses, three gardens and a municipal brick kiln. Open Sat & Sun 10am-4pm (last entrance 3.40pm).

Listen to the Bells

Astronomical clock

Every hour from morning until night, you can go to The astronomical clock on the Old Town Hall in the Old Town Square for the 'Procession of the Apostles'. For five minutes, 12 apostles nod as they pass over the clock on the hour as a bell rings. The clock dates back to 1410 when it was made by clockmaker Mikuláš of Kadaň and Jan Šindel, then later a professor of mathematics and astronomy at Charles University. The best time to visit is 9am or 10am when crowds are less dense.

Visit Prague Castle for free

Prague Castle

The Prague Castle was founded in 880 by Prince Bořivoj of the house of Premyslides. It houses St. George Basilica - the oldest sacral building of the Prague Castle.

Many don't realise that to walk around the grounds, and even into St Vitus Cathedral is free and glorious saving you $15 on the entry fee plus you can can watch the changing of the guard; the best show is performed daily at noon.

If you want to go inside there are three kinds of tickets for Prague Castle (each valid for two days), which allow entry:

A. Tour A 350Kč $15 St Vitus Cathedral, Old Royal Palace, Story of Prague Castle, Basilica of St George, Powder Tower, Golden Lane, Daliborka and Rosenberg Palace.

B. Tour B - 250Kč $10 St Vitus Cathedral, Old Royal Palace, Basilica of St George, Golden Lane and Daliborka.

C. Tour C 350Kč $15 St Vitus Treasury and Prague Castle

The Nový Svět Quarter is an alternative to Prague Castle's

Church Hop

Not only exceptional architecturally and historically, Pragues churches contain exquisite art, artefacts and other priceless treasures. Best of all, entry to most churches in Prague (except St Nicholas Church in Malá Strana) are free, as are the beautiful Wallenstein Garden and imposing Vyšehrad Citadel.

Here are the best of the free crop: Church of Our Lady Victorious. Church. St. George's Basilica at Prague Castle. St. Vitus Cathedral at Prague Castle (go to see the gorgeous stained glass), Mala Strana. St. Martin in the Wall Church. St. Salvator Church at Charles Bridge. Bethlehem Chapel.

Visit Municipal House

You'll have to pay for a guided tour of the Municipal House, a
celebrated concert house but you can walk through the gorgeous
art-nouveau cafe, the lobby and to the downstairs American Bar
without paying for admission.

Visit the Strahov Library

Set on the side of Prague Castle, there is a beautiful monastery. You can visit the beautiful library inside for just 100Kc - $4USD. There you can admire the incredible architecture of the building. But Go ONLY at 9am to avoid heaving crowds.

Visit the John Lennon Wall

Lennon was a hero to the youth of the Czech Republic during the totalitarian regime. The wall is not only a memorial to John Lennon, the graffiti and the poems are symbols of the pacific war against the communist regime that ruled the Czech Republic until 1989.

Relax in the Parks

Pause for a break after long hours of walking, or listen to local street musicians, either way go to Letná Park to relax in nature and take in great views. From the top of the park you can see the Vltava River and the bridges. Other great parks to relax in include Vojan Gardens and Kampa park.

Explore Street art

Prague has colorful murals and graffiti art displayed throughout the city. Murals sometimes cover up entire buildings and symbolise recent and historical events and topics. Go to the metro station Vltavská on line C. Built in the communist '80s, there's a lot of revealing street art to explore here.

Explore the markets

Coffee (káva) and tea (čaj)

Pragues markets are a fun and eye-opening plunge into local culture and, unless you succumb to the persistent vendors, it will cost you nothing. There is the famous Farmer's Market Náplavka by the Vltava River but prices are high. Head to the Farmer's Market Jiřího z Poděbrad and try cheap local snacks, drinks, and fruits. Its open Wednesday, Thursday, Fridays and Saturdays 8 AM to 2 PM.

Visit Petrín Hill

Across from U Svejku is the funicular station to Petrín Hill. Costing 12Kc - $0.20, the funicular trip takes five minutes. Once atop climb Petrín Tower for phenomenal views over the whole of Prague. There are lots of benches and green space to enjoy a picnic on, so pack some tasty fare from one of the bakeries to enjoy with the view.

Food and drink tips

Eat the best cakes in Prague

The best cakes in Prague come from **Erhartova Curkrárna** in the Vinohrady area. You will not regret a visit there.
Address: Vinohradská 2022/125, 130 00 Vinohrady

Best bang for your buck all-you-can-eat

Indian by Nature offers an all you can eat for $7.
All you can eat buffets are a great way to stock on on nutritious food while travelling. Don't drink much water or eat bread and you'll get more than your money's worth.
Address: Pernerova 478/1, 186 00 Karlín.

Cheap beers

If you don't go out you'll miss out on some great venues – the clubs and bars make it hard to catch some sleep in Prague. **Bar 69** is one of the cheapest pubs with great beer. 31 kč for 0,5L of Kozel - -$1.

Address: Navrátilova 666/7

Letná Zahradní restaurace has a leafy outdoor beer garden with great views and cheap beers - $1.50.

A great place to get lost is 'Vinárna U Sudu' just off Wenceslas Square in the New Town. This traditional Czech pub never seems to end.

Karlovy Lazne is a nightclub with five floors playing different music, its a great for cheap partying. Go before 22:00 for free entry.

INSIDER CULTURAL INSIGHT

A Prague local drinks are average of 155 litres of beers a year.

Is the tap water drinkable?

Tap water in Prague is perfectly safe to drink.

Haggle-o-meter

How much can you save haggling here?

Gentle haggling is common at markets in Prague. Haggling in stores is generally unacceptable, although some good-humoured bargaining at smaller artisan or craft shops is not unusual if you are making multiple purchases.

Enjoy your first Day for under $10

Start the day with a jug of tea or coffee and a bagel in Káva Káva Káva. Then get tram #18 from Narodni trida (just up from Káva) to 'Prazsky hrad' (Prague Castle). Catch the changing of the guard before exploring the castle. Visit St Vitus Cathedral, one of Europe's most magnificent, and exit the castle through 'Golden Lane'. Walk down the castle steps, taking in views over the Vltava. Make your way down to U Svejku on Ujezd for some lunch and try a Trdelník (rolled pastry) from a street vendor. Visit St Nicholas' Church. Marvel at the fresco on the ceiling. Cross Charles Bridge en route to the Old Town Square. Watch the 'Procession of the Apostles' at the astronomical clock. Finish the night off with some street stand sausages and beers while watching the sunset in Letná Park.

Websites to save you Money

1. **TalkTalkbnb.com** - Here you stay for free when you teach the host your native language
2. Rome2Rio.com - the go to site for good travel prices on train, bus, planes etc. Especially good for paths less travelled.
3. GoEuro.com - the best travel site in Europe.
4. couchsurfing.com - stay for free with a local - always check reviews.
5. trustedhousesitter.com - always check reviews
6. booking.com - now sends you vouchers for discounts in the city when you book through them
7. blablacar.com - travel in car with locals already going to your destination
8. airbnb.com for both accommodation and experiences.
9. hostelbookers.com - book hostels
10. http://www.neweuropetours.eu/prague - free walking tour
11. https://www.slevomat.cz/daily-deals-in-prague - daily deals sites.

Need to Know

Currency: Czech Crowns

Language: Czech.

Money: Widely available ATMs.

Visas: http://www.doyouneedvisa.com/

Time: GMT + 1

When to Go

High Season: July and August.

Shoulder: May, April, June

Low Season: September to May.

Important Numbers

113 Ambulance

112 Police

Watch to understand the History

Prague 's history is fascinating. There are tons of documentaries. This is a great in-depth one - https://www.youtube.-com/watch?v=HU7ZFmg1zus

Cheapest route to Prague from America

At the time of writing Norwegian are flying direct for around $400 return out of Boston. I specialise in finding cheap flights, so if you need help finding a cheap flight simply review this book and send me an email. philgtang@gmail.com

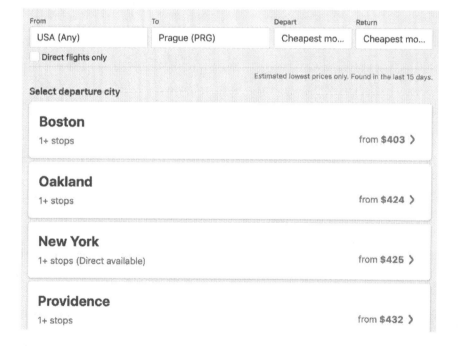

Cheap Eats

Fill your stomach without emptying your wallet by trying these local restaurants with mains under $5.

(Download the offline map on google maps, (instructions 1. go to app 2. select offline apps in the left sidebar 3. go to the area you want to download 4. click download). Then simply type the restaurant names in to navigate, star them so you can see where the cheap eats are when you're out and about to avoid wasting your money at hyped tourist joints)

Cafe Merkur
Tradtiional Czech food on the cheap.

Johnny Pizza
Delicious cheap Italian Pizza.

Sad Man's Tongue Bar & Bistro
International European Pub with low prices.

Creme De La Creme
The best ice cream in the city.

Cafe Na hlas
Breakfast for two $10.

Da Tarquinio
More Delicious cheap Italian Pizza.

Nase maso
Tiny place, awesome meatloaf.

Bistro & Bar
Best falafel and hummus in Prague.

ROESEL
Great cheap craft beer & cake

Mr.HotDoG
American Gastropub with cheap Comfort food.

BARFuD
Best burger in Prague

DEN NOC
Perfect Traditional Czech food.

Yori Restaurant
Cheap Thai Vietnamese food.

More Vietnamese food: Banh Mi Ba, Mr. Banh Mi, Café 79

More Gelato: Angelato, Puro Gelato

TIP: Couvert is charged (to cover bread and condiments); this should be clearly marked on the menu but if you receive a bread basket when you sit down expect to be charged for it.

Avoid these tourist traps or scams

Scams and trickery are the scourge of a traveler's budget/ Beware of extremely helpful strangers. If someone approaches you and you fear their intentions just say 'sorry, no english.' and walk on.

There are **pickpockets** lurking around the crowded attractions. Don't keep things in your back pockets in this or any other busy area or crowded pubs - they are opportunistic thieves rather than forceful ones.

Fake Charity Petition: You're at a popular sight when someone thrusts a petition at you. It's likely a woman or a teen who, often pretending to be deaf, will try to get you to sign an official-looking petition, supposedly in support of a charity (the petition is often in English, which should be a clue). The petitioner then demands a cash donation.

Phony Police: Two thieves in uniform — posing as Tourist Police — stop you on the street, flash there bogus badges, and ask to check your wallet. You won't even notice some bills are missing until after they leave. Never give your wallet to anyone. If this happens to you politely decline and if they are persistent inform them that you need to phone the police to check their identities.

Basic Phrases

Děkuji, which means thank you will be appreciated by servers.

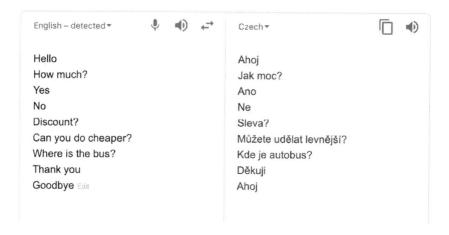

English – detected ▾	Czech ▾
Hello	Ahoj
How much?	Jak moc?
Yes	Ano
No	Ne
Discount?	Sleva?
Can you do cheaper?	Můžete udělat levnější?
Where is the bus?	Kde je autobus?
Thank you	Děkuji
Goodbye Edit	Ahoj

Getting out

Train
Booking ahead can save you up to 90% of the cost of the ticket but even with the discount the bus is much cheaper.

Bus
Regiojet is the cheapest bus from Prague. Use rome2rio.com to find the best deal.

Plane

At the time of writing Ryanair are offering the cheapest flights onwards. Take advantage of discounts and specials. Sign up for e-newsletters from local carriers including Ryanair to learn about special fares. Be careful with cheap airlines, most will allow hand-luggage only, and some charge for anything that is not a backpack. Check their websites before booking if you need to take luggage.

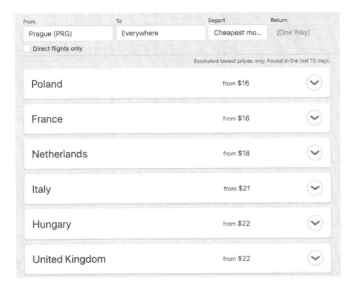

RECAP: How to have a $1,000 trip to Prague on a $180 budget

Five star hotels
Last minute 5 star hotels deals. Check on the same day of your stay for cheap five star hotel deals. Go to booking.com enter Prague, tonight, only one night and filter by 5 stars. This can be very effective on the weekends in the low season when hotels empty of their business travellers. Potential saving $800.

Try blind booking
The cheapest hotel deals are available when you 'blind book'. You don't know the name of the hotel before you book. Use Last Minute Top Secret hotels and you can find a four star hotel from $30 a night in Prague! lastminute.com/hotel/prague

Book a nice Airbnb 3 months in advance
You can find a central Airbnb in the city from $9 a night when you book at least 3 months in advance.

Restaurant deals
Nearly every restaurant in Prague offers a midday menu for lunch at around 7€ If you're on a budget, but like eating out, consider doing your dining in the daytime. Potential saving $100.

Go to museums/ attractions on their free days
Get cultured for free, or for cheap, by knowing the gallery and museum discount days. The average traveller spends $80 on museums in Prague, but there's an abundance of free or cheap attractions that are just as amazing. Potential saving $80.

Personal Cost Breakdown

	How	Cost normally	Cost when following suggested tip
How I got from the airport to the city	Bus	$25 Taxi	$2
Where I stayed	airbnb in the city - https://www.airbnb.com/rooms/21727317?s=51 $9	Hotels start at $90 a night	$27 for 3 nights
Tastiest street foods I ate and cost	Trdelník. Sausages (Klobásy) Mulled Wine. Fried Cheese Sandwich. Potatoes on a Stick.	You don't have to spend a lot to eat amazing food in Prague.	$3 average for a meal
How I got around	Bike, walk and metro	Travel on tram 22 - its lovely to sit back and watch the sights whirl by	$5
What I saw and paid	Churches, castles, architecture, Palace, museums, galleries	You can enjoy a lot in Prague for free	Palace entrance $15
My onward flight	Paris	Book six weeks ahead to get the lowest price.	$18
My Total costs			$100

The secret to saving HUGE amounts of money when travelling to Prague is...

Your mindset. Money is an emotional topic, if you associate words like cheapskate, Miser (and its £9.50 to go into Charles Dickens London house, oh the Irony) with being thrifty when travelling you are likely to say 'F-it' and spend your money needlessly because you associate pain with saving money. You pay now for an immediate reward. Our brains are prehistoric; they focus on surviving day to day. Travel companies and hotels know this and put trillions into making you believe you will be happier when you spend on their products or services. Our poor brains are up against outdated programming and an onslaught of advertisements bombarding us with the message: spending money on travel equals PLEASURE. To correct this carefully lodged propaganda in your frontal cortex you need to imagine your future self.

Saving money does not make you a cheapskate. It makes you smart. How do people get rich? They invest their money. They don't go out and earn it; they let their money earn more money. So every time you want to spend money, imagine this: while you travel your money is working for you, not you for money. While you sleep the money you've invested is going up and up. That's a pleasure a pricey entrance fee can't give you. Thinking about putting your money to work for you tricks your brain into believing you are not withholding pleasure from yourself, you are saving your money to invest so you can go to even more amazing places. You are thus turning thrifty travel into a pleasure fueled sport.

When you've got money invested - If you want to splash your cash on a first-class airplane seat - you can. I can't tell you how to invest your money, only that you should. Saving $20 on taxi's doesn't seem like much but over time you could be saving upwards of $15,000 a year, which is a deposit for a house which you can rent on Airbnb to finance more travel. Your brain making money looks like your brain on cocaine, so tell yourself saving money is making money.

Scientists have proved that imagining your future self is the easiest way to associate pleasure with saving money. You can download FaceApp — which will give you a picture of what you will look like older and greyer, or you can take a deep breath just before spending money and ask yourself if you will regret the purchase later.

The easiest ways to waste money travelling are:

Getting a taxi. The solution to this is to always download the google map before you go. Many taxi drivers will drive you around for 15 minutes when the place you were trying to get to is a 5-minute walk… remember while not getting an overpriced taxi to tell yourself, 'I am saving money to free myself for more travel.'
Spending money on overpriced food when hungry. The solution: carry snacks. A banana and an apple will cost you, in most places less than a dollar.
Spending on entrance fees to top-rated attractions. If you really want to do it, spend the money happily. If you're conflicted sleep on it. I don't regret spending $200 on a skydive over the Great Barrier Reef, I do regret going to the top of the shard in London for $60. Only you can know but make sure it's your decision and not the marketing directors at said top-rated attraction.
Telling yourself 'you only have the chance to see/eat/experience it now'. While this might be true, make sure YOU WANT to spend the money. Money spent is money you can't invest, and often you can have the same experience for much less.

You can experience luxurious travel on a small budget which will trick your brain into thinking you're already a high-roller, which will mean you'll be more likely to start acting like one and invest your money. Stay in five-star hotels for $5 by booking on the day of your stay on booking.com to enjoy last minute deals. You can go to fancy restaurants using daily deal sites. Ask your airline about last minute upgrades to first-class or business. I paid $100 extra on a $179 ticket to Cuba from Germany to be bumped to Business Class. When you ask you will be surprised what you can get both at hotels and airlines.

Travel, as the saying goes is the only thing you spend money on that makes you richer. In practice, you can easily waste money, making it difficult to enjoy that metaphysical wealth. The biggest money saving secret is to turn bargain hunting into a pleasurable activity, not an annoyance. Budgeting consciously can be fun, don't feel disappointed because you don't spend the $60 to go into an attraction, feel good because soon that $60 will soon be earning money for you. Meaning, you'll have the time and money to enjoy more metaphysical wealth, while your bank balance increases.

FREE BOOK

GET ANY 2020 SUPER CHEAP GUIDE FREE

REVIEW THIS GUIDE TO RECEIVE THE 2020 EDITION OF ANY SUPER CHEAP GUIDE **FREE**. Go to

with a screenshot of your review to claim YOUR FREE book.

So there it is, you can save a small fortune by being strategic with your trip planning. We've arranged everything in the guide to offer the best bang for your buck. Which means we took the view that if it's not a good investment for your money, we wouldn't include it. Why would a guide called 'Super Cheap' include lots of overpriced attractions? That said if you think we've missed something or have unanswered questions ping me an email philgtang@gmail.com I'm on central Europe time and usually reply within 8 hours of getting your mail.

Don't put your dreams off!

Time is a currency you never get back and travel is its greatest return on investment. Plus now you know you can visit Prague for a fraction of the price most would have you believe.

Winter view of Prague's old Town

Prague Metro Map

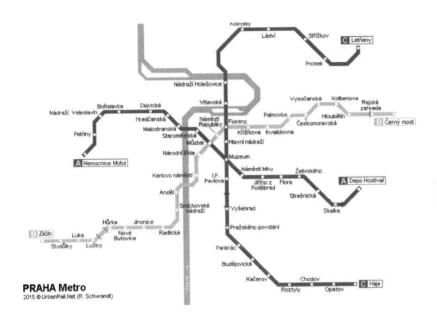

PRAHA Metro
2015 © UrbanRail.Net (R. Schwandl)

Thank you for reading

Dear Lovely Reader,

If you have found this book useful, please consider writing a short review on Amazon.

One person from every 1000 readers leaves a review on Amazon. It would mean more than you could ever know if you were one of our 1 in 1000 people to take the time to write a short review.

We are a group of four friends who all met travelling 15 years ago. We believe that great experiences don't need to blow your budget, just your mind.

Thank you so much for reading again and for spending your time and investing your trips future in Super Cheap Guides Guides.

Phil

P.S If you need any more super cheap tips we'd love to hear from you e-mail me at philgtang@gmail.com, we have a lot of contacts in every region, so if there's a specific bargain you're hunting we can help you find it :-)

GET 300 TRAVEL GUIDES FULL OF SUPER CHEAP TIPS FREE ON AMAZON WITH KINDLE UNLIMITED.

UNCOVERED A SUPER CHEAP TIP DURING YOUR TRAVELS? GET PAID FOR IT. EMAIL PHILGTANG@GMAIL.COM

WE PAY FOR TIPS

CHOOSE FROM PRO RATA ROYALTIES OR A $50 AMAZON VOUCHER

Bonus Budget Travel Hacks

I've included these bonus travel hacks to help you plan and enjoy the trip cheaply, joyfully and smoothly.

How NOT to be ripped off

The thrill of spontaneity is incredible, but if you do a little planning ahead, you will not only save yourself from several mental troubles, but also a lot of money. I am the laziest of planners when it comes to travelling, but I make sure I begin a trip well.

1. **Never ever agree to pay as much as you want trap. Always decide on a price before.**

Whoever you're dealing with is trained to tell you, they are uninterested in money! This is a trap. If you let people do this they will ask for MUCH MORE money at the end, and because you have used there service, you will feel obliged to pay. This is a conman's trick and nothing more.

2. Choose to stay in a hostel, instead of a hotel the first nights to get the lay of the land.

get a chance to learn so much. I have also observed that the location of hostels is often close to main attractions. Also please do not worry about luxury, you are going to spend most of your time outside anyway.

3. Pack light

You can move faster and easier. If you take heavy luggage so you will end up taking cabs which are comparatively very costly.

4. If a local approaches you, they are normally trying to scam you, this is ALWAYS true in tourist destinations.

5. Don't book for more than two days and note down the address on your phone

Unless the place you're doing is going to be busy. e.g Alaska in summer.

6. Withdraw cash from ATM's when you need it, don't carry it with you.

5. NEVER use the airport taxi service. Plan to use public transport before you reach the airport

6. Don't buy a sim card from the airport, but from the local supermarkets it will be 50% less.

7. Eat at local restaurants serving regional food
Food defines culture. Exploring all delights available to the palate.

How to overcome travel related struggles

Anxiety when flying

It has been over 40 years since a plane has been brought down because of turbulence. 40 years! Planes are built to withstand lighting strikes, extreme storms and ultimately can adjust course to get out of their way. Landing and take over are when the most accidents happen, but you have statistically three times the chance of winning a huge jackpot lottery, then you do of crashing then.

If you feel afraid on the flight focus on your breathing saying the word 'smooth' over and over until the flight is smooth. Always check the airline safety record airlinerating.com I was surprised to learn Ryanair and Easyjet as much less safe than Wizz Air according to those ratings. If there is extreme turbulence, I feel much better knowing I'm in a 7 star safety plane.

Wanting to sleep instead of seeing new places

This is a common problem. Just relax, there's little point doing fun things when you feel tired. Plan and fact in jetlag.

Going over budget

Come back from a trip to a monster credit card bill? You're not alone. These are the costs that can crept up. Don't let them.

- To and from the airport. Solution: leave adequate time and take the cheapest method - book before.
- Baggage. Solution: take hand luggage and post things you might need to yourself.
- Eating out. Solution: go to cheap eats places and suggest those to friends.
- Parking. Solution: use apps to find free parking
- Tipping. Solution Leave a modest tip and tell the server you will write them a nice review.
- Souvenirs. Solution: fridge magnets only.
- Giving to the poor. (This one still gets me, but if you're giving away $10 a day - it adds up) Solution: volunteer your time at a local soup kitchens.

Price v Comfort

I love traveling, I don't love struggling. I like decent accommodation, being able to eat properly and see places and enjoy. I am never in the mood for low cost airlines or crappy transfers so here's what I do to save money.

- Avoid organised tours unless you are going to a place where safety is a real issue. They are expensive and constrain your wanderlust to typical things. Note, I only recommend them in Algeria, Iran and Papua New Guinea - where language and gender views pose serious problems all cured by a reputable tour organiser.
- Eat what the locals do.
- Cook in your airbnb/ hostel where restaurants are expensive.
- Shop at local markets.
- Never take the first price.

- Spend time choosing your flight, and check the operator on ari-lineratings.com
- Mix up hostels and Airbnbs. Hostels for meeting people, Airbnb for relaxing and feeling 'at home'.

Not knowing where toilets are

Use Toilet Finder - https://play.google.com/store/apps/details?id=com.bto.toilet&hl=en

Your airbnb is awful

Airbnb customer service is notoriously bad. Help yourself out. Never book somewhere without at least 5 reviews. Try to sort things out with the host, but if you can't take photos of everything e.g bed, bathroom, mess, doors, contact them within 24 hours and tell them you had to leave and pay for new accommodation. And ask politely for a full refund.

The airline loses your bag

Take a photo of your checked luggage before you check it.
Go to the Luggage desk before leaving the airport and report the bag missing.
Most airlines will give you an overnight bag, ask where your staying and return the bag to you within three days. Its extremely rare for them to completely lose it these days, but if that happens you should submit an insurance claim.

Your travel companion lets you down.

Whether it's a breakup or a friend cancelling, it sucks and can ramp up costs. In these cases, I normally go to a well-reviewed hostel and find someone I want to travel with - if I need someone to cover the extra costs.

Culture shock

I had one of the strongest culture shocks while spending 6 months in Japan. It was overwhelming how much I actually had to prepare when I went outside of the door (googling words and sentences what to use, where to go, which station and train line to use, what is this food called in Japanese and how does its look etc.). I was so tired constantly but in the end I just let go and went with my extremely bad Japanese. I was trying to ask for soup one day and asked for help with my piles... the people were laughing so hard one actually choked.

If you feel culture shocked its because your brain is referencing your surroundings to what you know. My tip is to just let go and learn some of the local language. You won't like everywhere you go - but you can at least relax everywhere you go.

You're tired

I feel like I just want to go go go go go and See everything and don't let myself just take some time to rest without feeling guilty or conflicted but its important to rest when travelling. I like to create a mini entertainment zone, and occasionally binge watch something or watch documentaries about where I currently am on YouTube.

Car rental

I always use carrentals.com and book with a credit card. Most credit cards will give you free insurance for the car, so you don't need to pay the extra.

You're sick

First off ALWAYS, purchase travel insurance. Including emergency transport up to $500k even to back home, which is usually less than $10 additional. I use https://www.comparethemarket.com/travel-insurance/

If I am sick I normally check into a hotel with room service and ride it out.

Make a Medication Travel Kit

Take medications with you, it is always more expensive to buy there unless you are lucky.

- Antidiarrheal medication (for example, bismuth subsalicylate, loperamide)
- Antihistamine.
- Anti-motion sickness medication.
- Medicine for pain or fever (such as acetaminophen, aspirin, or ibuprofen)
- Mild laxative.
- Cough suppressant/expectorant.
- Throat Lozenges

Save yourself from most travel related hassle

- Do not screw around with immigration and customs staff. You will lose.

- Book the most direct flight you can find, nonstop if possible. Keep weather in mind with connecting flights and watch out for connections in cities with multiple airports through different airports (airlines sometimes connect this way... watch it in places like London and New York)

- Carry a US$ 100 bill for emergency cash. I have entered a country and all ATM and credit card systems were down. US$ can be exchanged nearly anywhere in the world.

- Pack light. Pack light. Pack light. Pack light.

- On long connections, many airport lounges are pay lounges and can be very comfortable and cheaper than a transit hotel.

- Check, and recheck, required visas and such BEFORE the day of your trip. Some countries, for instance, require a ticket out of the country in order to enter. Others, like the US and Australia, require electronic authorization in advance.

- McDonalds and Starbucks offer free wifi in most of the world.

- Security is asinine and inconsistent around the world. Keep this in mind when connecting flights. Always leave at least 2 hours for international connections or international to domestic.

- Expats are rarely the best source for local information. Lots of barstool pontificates in the world.

- Wiki travel is perfect to use for a lay of the land

- Expensive luggage rarely lasts longer than cheap luggage, in my experience. Fancy leather bags are usually toast with air travel.

- Buy travel insurance. A comprehensive annual policy is best and not that expensive.

- Learning to say please and thank you in the local language is not that hard and opens doors. As does a smile and a handshake.

Where and How to Make Friends

Become popular at the airport

Want to become popular at the airport? Pack a power bar with multiple outlets and just see how many friends you make. It's amazing how many people forget their chargers, or who packed them in the luggage that they checked in!

Stay in Hostels

I note there's a line about backpacking, young, confident, hostel demographic that seems to have a whole unspoken backstory going on.

First of all, Hostels don't have to be shared dorms, and they cater to a much wider demographic than is assumed in the OP's comments. In my experience hostels were a way better environment for meeting people than hotels, and more importantly they tended to open up excursion opportunities that further opened up that opportunity. Hotel guests tend to be more cocooned, either couples or families, or if solo, more often than not business travellers, who are rarely interested in chit-chat.

Or take up a hobby

However, if hostels are a definite no-no; find an interest. Take up a hobby where you will meet people. I've dived for years and the nature of diving is you're always paired up with a dive buddy, and I met a lot of interesting people that way. Find something like that the gets people together. However, all of this is about creating the opportunity, you still have to take it, and if you're not the most outgoing person, pack the power supply.

GENERAL HACKS

From saving space in your suitcase to scoring cheap flights, there are a wealth of travel hacks that can help you use to have a stress-free and happy travels without breaking the bank.

Planning and booking stages of travel are equally instrumental in how successful your trip will be, which can be a lot of pressure.

Before You Go

Money

- Get cash from ATMs for best rates.
- Never change at airport exchange desks unless you absolutely have to, then just change enough to get to an ATM.
- Charles Schwab High Yield Checking accounts refund every single ATM fee worldwide, require no minimum balance and have no monthly fee.
- Bring a spare credit card for real emergencies.
- Split cash in various places on your person (pockets, shoes) and in your luggage.
- Use a money belt under your clothes or put $50 in your shoe/ bra incase.

Food
-
- When it comes to food, eat in local restaurants, not tourist-geared joints or choose a hostel.
- with facilities and cook for yourself. The same goes for drinking and going out.

- Bring boiled eggs, canned tuna and nuts with you to avoid being caught out by extreme hunger and having to buy expensive/ unhealthy foods full of sugar.
- Take a spork - a knife, spoon and fork all in one.

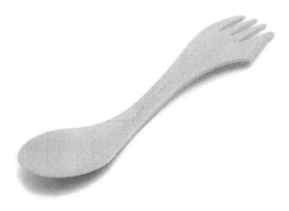

Water Bottle

Take a water bottle with a filter. We love these ones from Water to Go.
Empty it before airport security and seperate the two pieces.

Bug Sprays

Always buy on Amazon. If you have an urgent need while travelling you will pay over the odds. If you are especially tasty to mosquitoes spray your clothes with Permethrin before you travel. A 'Bite Away' zapper can be used after the bite to totally erase it. It cuts down on the itching and need for anti-hestimaines

Order free mini's

Don't buy those expensive travel sized toiletries, order travel sized freebies online. This gives you the opportunity to try brands you've never used before, and who knows, you might even find your new favourite soap.

CHEAP FLIGHT HACKS

Use skyscanner.net - they include the low-cost airlines that others like Kayak leave out.

Use open parameters, e.g if you want to fly from Chicago to Paris, put in USA to France, you may find flights from NYC to Paris for $70 and can take a cheap flight to NYC. Calculate full costs, including accommodation and getting to and from airports before bookting.

ALWAYS USE A PRIVATE BROWSER TO BOOK FLIGHTS

Skyscanner and other sites track your IP address and put prices up and down based on what they determine your desire to buy. e.g if you've booked one-way and are looking for the return these sites will jack the prices up by in most cases 50%. Incognito browsing pays.

Use a VPN such as Hola to book your flight from your destination

Install Hola, change your destination, the location from which a ticket is booked can affect the price. Try using a different address when booking to take advantage of this.

Choose the right time to buy your ticket.

Choose the right time to buy your ticket, as purchasing tickets on a Sunday has been proven to be cheaper. If you can only book during the week, try to do it on a Tuesday.

Fly late for cheaper prices.

Fly late for cheaper prices. Red-eye flights, the ones that leave last in the day, are typically cheaper and less crowded, so aim to book that flight if possible. You will also get through the airport much quicker at the end of the day.

PRO TIP: Get an empty water bottle with you. Once you pass the security check, fill it with water. It will save you $5

Use this APP for same day flights

The Get the Flight Out app (iOS only) from fare tracker Hopper is a go-to choice for travelers looking for same-day flights. The inventory is from major airlines as well as low-cost carriers, and the prices are always favorable. A recent search found a British Airways round-trip from JFK Airport to London's Heathrow for $300.

Take a waterproof bag

If you're travelling alone you can swim without worrying about your phone, wallet and passport laying on the beach.

You can also use it as a source of entertainment on those ultra budget flights

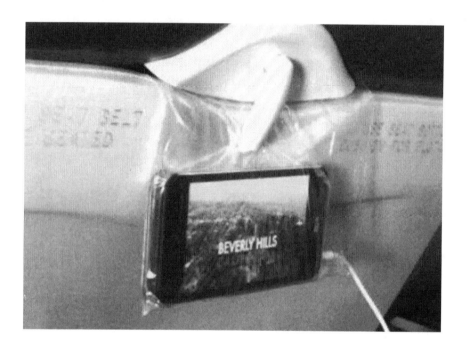

Make a private entertainment centre anywhere

Always take an eye-mask, earplugs, a scarf and a kindle reader - so you can sleep and entertain yourself anywhere!

Take a sponge with you – freeze sponges to keep your food treats fresh.

As long as they are completely frozen, you won't have any problems getting them through airport security.

Travel Gadgets

The door alarm

If you're nervous and staying in private rooms or airbnbs take a door alarm. For those times when you just don't feel safe. 'When you're in a new place, an added measure of protection can give you peace of mind to sleep.

Smart Blanket

I used it when flying to Zurich. The plane was freezing, and there were no blankets to be had. I was the only one that was warm and cozy for the whole 8 hours. Amazon http://amzn.to/2hTYIOP I paid $49.00

The coat that becomes a tent

https://www.adiff.com/products/tent-jacket

Clever Tank Top with Secret Pockets

Keep your valuables safe in this top. Perfect for all climates. https://www.amazon.com/Clever-Travel-Companion-Unisex-secret/dp/B00O94PXLE

Buy on Amazon for $39.90

Convenient Water Bottle with Built-in Pill Organizer

Great way to take your medication while on the go. The medication holder can also be detached. Holding 23 oz. or 600ml, the bottle cap also doubles as a cup. Ingenious!

Optical Camera Lens for Smartphones and Tablets

Leave your bulky camera at home. Turn your device into a high-performance camera. Buy on Amazon for $9.95

Travel-sized Wireless Router with USB Media Storage

Convert any wired network to a wireless network. Buy on Amazon for $17.99

Buy a Scrubba Bag to wash your clothes on the go

Or a cheaper imitable. You can wash your clothes on the go.

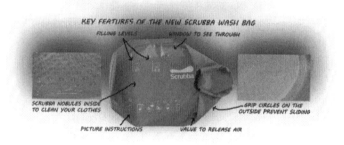

On The Road

Follow locals

Follow the locals. If there are locals around you, you're doing it right. If there are only tourists, you're probably being ripped off.

Set-up a New Uber/ other car hailing app account for discounts

Google offers $50 free for new users in most cities when you have a new gmail.com email account.

Couchsurfing

Totally safe when the person has reviews, but competitive. Book early and confirm before you go. Take a tent, you'll have somewhere to stay if the host cancels last minute.

Hitch-hiking

A good option to save money on transport which will take up a much larger chunk of your budget but only do in groups and let someone know when you are at all times. Family locator app is a good way to do this automatically.

Internet

Check Foursquare for free Wi-Fi hotspots
Get a local cheap sim for data on the go.
Rewards lounges usually have unprotected Wi-Fi networks.
Buying Internet access from your mobile device rather than your laptop can get you a better rate. Alternatively, you can spoof your browser's User Agent.

Include external portable power battery for phone charging

Look for people already eating and drinking

Check the Spotted by Locals apps or blogs (Europe & North America)
Get the local experiences: Trip: The Happiest Way to Enjoy Truly Local Experiences (Trip is now available in 86 countries)

Checking Bags

Everyone says this, but it's always worth saying again: Never, ever check a bag if you possibly can avoid it. You're better off doing laundry a couple times in a hostel bathroom. You might also meet interesting people at a coin-op laundry.

Make sure to take a photo of your bag before you check it. This will speed up the paperwork if it is damaged or lost.

Take advantage of other hotel's amenities

Take advantage of other hotel's amenities, for example, if you fancy a swim but you're nowhere near the ocean, try the nearest hotel with a pool. As long as you buy a drink, the hotel staff will likely grant you access.

Fill up your mini bar for free.

Fill up your mini bar for free by storing things from the breakfast bar in your mini bar to give you a greater selection of drinks and food.

Save yourself some ironing

Save yourself some ironing by using the steam from the shower to get rid of wrinkles in clothing. If something is creased, leave it trapped with the steam in the bathroom overnight for even better results.

Recover from a big night out.

Recover from a big night out by using a pants hanger to secure the curtains, keeping your room nice and dark.

See somewhere else for free!

See somewhere else for free! Check to see if your flight offers free stopovers, allowing you to experience another city without spending any extra money.

Wear your heaviest clothes

on the plane to save weight in your suitcase, allowing you to bring more with you. Big coats can then be used as pillows to make your flight more comfortable.

Rebook for a cheaper change of flight.

Some airlines charge high changing fees, whereas last minute flights can be extremely cheap.

Google Your Flight Number before you leave for the airport

Easily find out where your plane is from anywhere. Confirm the status of your flight before you leave.

Protect your belongings during the flight.

Put a 'Fragile' on anything you check to ensure that it's handled better as it goes through security. It'll also be one of the first bags released after the flight, getting you out of the airport quicker.

Don't get lost while you're away.

Find where you want to go using Google Maps, then type 'OK Maps' into the search bar to store this information for offline viewing.

Dine Early

Walk-ins are often accommodated late in the afternoon, and reservations at buzzy restaurants are more plentiful then, too and lunch deals can be half the price of dinner.

Use car renting services

Drive Now or Car2Go.

Share Rides

Use sites like blablacar.com to find others who are driving in your direction. It can be 80% cheaper than normal transport. Just check the drivers reviews.

Use free gym passes

Get a free gym day pass by googling the name of a local gym and free day pass.

When asked by people providing you a service where you are from

If there's no price list for the service you are asking for, when asked where you are from, Say you are from a well-known poorer country. I normally say Macedonia, and if they don't know where it is, add it's a poor country. If you say UK, USA, the majority of Europe bar the well-known poorer countries taxi drivers, tour operators etc will match the price to what they think you pay at home

Hacks for Families

Rent an Airbnb apartment so you can cook

Apartments are much better for families, as you have all the amenities you'd have at home. They are normally cheaper per person too.

Shop at local markets

Eat seasonal products and local products. Get closer to the local market and observe the prices and the offer. What you can find more easily, will be the cheapest

Take Free Tours

Download free podcast tours of the destination you are visiting. The podcast will tell you where to start, where to go, and what to look for. Often you can find multiple podcast tours of the same place. Listen to all of them if you like, each one will tell you a little something new.

Pack Extra Ear Phones

If you go on a museum tour, they often have audio guides. Instead of having to rent one for each person, take some extra earphones. Most audio tour devices have a place to plug in a second set.

Free Hotel Breakfast

Only stay at hotels that include a free breakfast with their standard rate. If you are on a week-long family trip, this could save you a ton of money.

Buy Souvenirs Ahead of Time

If you are buying souvenirs someone touristy, you are paying a premium price. By ordering the same exact products online, you can save a lot of money.

Use Cheap Transportation

Do as the locals do, including weekly passes.

Carry a Reusable Water Bottle

Spending money on water and other beverages can quickly add up. Instead of paying for drinks, take some refillable water bottles.

Combine Attractions

Many major cities offer ticket bundles where one price gets you into 5 or 6 popular attractions. You will need to plan ahead of time to decide what things you plan to do on vacation and see if they are selling these activities together.

Pack Snacks

Granola bars, apples, baby carrots, bananas, cheese crackers, juice boxes, pretzels, fruit snacks, apple sauce, grapes, and veggie chips.

Stick to Carry-On Bags

Do not pay to check a large bag. Even a small child can pull a carry-on.

Visit free art galleries and museums

Just google the name + free days.

Eat Street Food

There's a lot of unnecessary fear around this. You can watch the food prepared. Go for the stands that have a steady queue.

Travel Gadgets for Families

Dropcam

Are what-if scenarios playing out in your head? Then you need Dropcam.

'Dropcam HD Internet Wi-Fi Video Monitoring Cameras help you watch what you love from anywhere. In less than a minute, you'll have it setup and securely streaming video to you over your home Wi-Fi. Watch what you love while away with Dropcam HD.'

Approximate Price: $139

Kelty-Child-Carrier

Voted as one of the best hiking essentials if you're traveling with kids and can carry a child up to 18kg.

Jetkids Bedbox

No more giving up your own personal space on the plane.

How to earn money WHILE travelling

1. Online english teaching job $20 - you will need a private room for this. - https://t.vipkid.com.cn/?refereeId=3262664
2. Work in a hostel. Normally you'll get some cash and free accommodation.
3. Fruit picking. I picked Bananas in Tully Australia for $20 an hour. The jobs are menial but can be quite meditative.
4. You could work on luxury yachts in the med. Its hard work, but you can save money - DesperateSailors.com
5. fiverr.com - offer a small service, like making a video template and changing the content for each buyer.
6. upwork.com - you need to put in a lot of work to make this successful, but if you have a unique skill like coding, or marketing it can be lucrative.
7. Make a udemy.com course
8. Use skype to deliver all manner of services, language lessons, therapy etc. Google for what you could offer. Most speclaisoms have a platform you can use to find clients and they will take a cut of your earnings/ require a fee.
9. Become an Airbnb experience host - but this requires you to know one place and stay there for a time. And you will need a work visa for that country.
10. WWOOF.org which focuses on organic farm work.
11. Rent your place out on airbnb while you travel and get a cleaner to manage it.

Safety

I always check fco.co.uk before travelling. NEVER RELY on websites or books. Things are changing constantly and the FCO's advice is always UP TO DATE and extremely conservative.

I've travelled alone to over 150 countries and the main thing I learnt is if you walk around scared, or anticipating you're going to be pickpocketed, your constant fear will attract bad energy. Murders or attacks on travellers are the mainstay of media, not reality, especially in countries familiar with travellers. The only place I had cause to genuinely fear for my life was Papa New Guinea - where nothing actually happened to me only my own panic over culture shock.

There are many things you can do to stop yourself being victim to the two main problems when travelling: theft or being scammed.

I will address theft first. Here are my top tips. Take these with a pinch of salt, I've written them whilst in India, which can be sketchy if you're travelling alone.

- Stay alert while you're out and always have an exit strategy (no alleyways when alone).
- Keep your money in a few different places on your person and your passport somewhere it can't be grabbed.
- Take a photo of your passport on your phone incase (I never lost of had mine stolen in 15 years of constant travel). If you do lose it, google for your embassy, you can usually get a temporary pretty fast.
- Google safety tips for traveling in your country to help yourself out and memorise the emergency number.
- At hostels keep your large bag in the room far under the bed/ out of the way with a lock on the zipper.

- I keep all money, valuables, passport, etc on me in my day bag. And at night I keep larger bag locked and my day bag in bed next to me/under my pillow depending on how secure the rest of the facilities are. I will alter any of the above based on circumstance or comfortability, for example, the presence of lockers or how many people in the room.
- On buses/trains I would definitely have a lock on the zippers of all bags and I would even lock it to the luggage rack if you want to sleep/if this is a notoriously sketchy route. Bag theft on Indian trains for example is very common.
- I hate constantly checking my bags and having anxiety over it. I bring a small lock for all zippers (with important things not in easily accessible pockets.
- Get a personal keychain alarm. The sound will scare anyone away.
- Don't wear any jewellery. A man attempted to rob a friend of her engagement ring in Bogota, Colombia, and in hindsight I wished I'd told her to leave it at home/wear it on a hidden necklace, as the chaos it created was avoidable.
- Don't hold your phone out while in the street.
- Don't turn your back to traffic while you use your phone.
- When traveling in the tuktuk sit in the middle and keep your bag secure. Wear sunglasses as dust can easily get in your eyes.
- Watch your bag - make sure your zippers are closed and you're aware of your things.
- Don't let anyone give you flowers, bracelets, or any type of trinket, even if they insist it's for free and compliment you like crazy.
- Be careful at night & while drinking.
- Don't go solo on excursions that take you away from crowds.
- Let someone know where you are if you are fearful. Use the family app.
- Don't let strangers know that you are alone - unless they are travel friends ;-) in fact, this is more for avoiding scams or men if you are a women travelling alone.
- Lastly, and most importantly -Trust your gut! If it doesn't feel right, it isn't.

Our Writers

Phil Tang has traveled a number of places using Lonely Planet guides and finds them to be incredibly useful; however, their recommendations for restaurants and accommodation are WAY OUT of my budget. Plus any estimation of cost was always widely inaccurate. So over the past 14 years I started compiling the Super Cheap Insider Guides-for people like me, who want a guide within a set budget, but one that doesn't compromise on fun.

Ali Blythe has been writing about amazing places for 17 years. He loves travel and especially tiny budgets equalling big adventures nearly as much as his family. He recently trekked the Satopanth Glacier trekking through those ways from where no one else would trek. A adventure by nature and bargainist by religion, his written over 200 guides for people travelling on a budget.

Michele Whitter writes about languages and travel. What separates her from other travel writers is her will to explain complex topics in a no-nonsense, straightforward manner. She doesn't promise the world. But always delivers step-by-step strategies you can immediately implement to travel on a small Budget.

Kim Mortmier whether it's a two-week, two-month, or two-year trip, Kim's input on Travel Addict Travel Guides show you how to stretch your money further so you can travel cheaper, smarter, and with more wanderlust. She loves going over land on horses.

Copyright

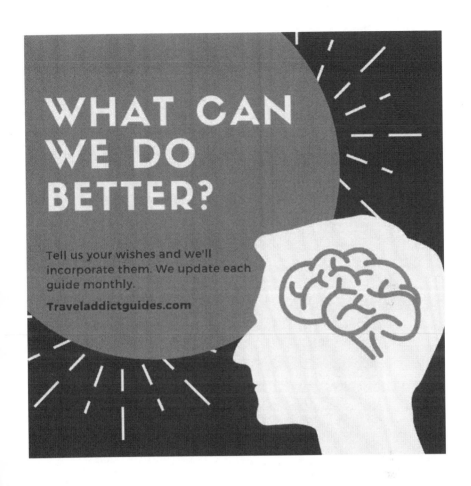

65435624R00064